- *Vol. 2* -
WORKING TOGETHER

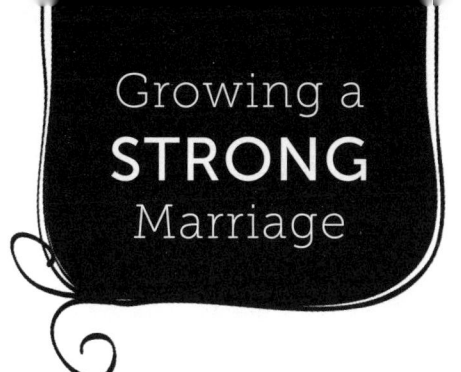

Growing a
STRONG
Marriage

Session 2-4 in first Book (handwritten)

– *Vol. 2* –
WORKING TOGETHER

STUDY GUIDE BY AMY MCGOWAN

HENDRICKSON
PUBLISHERS

Growing a Strong Marriage (Vol. 2)—Working Together

© 2015 Hendrickson Publishers Marketing, LLC
P. O. Box 3473
Peabody, Massachusetts 01961-3473

ISBN 978-1-61970-585-2

Unless otherwise indicated, Scripture quotations are from The Holy Bible, English Standard Version® (ESV®), copyright © 2001 by Crossway, a publishing ministry of Good News Publishers. Used by permission. All rights reserved.

Printed in the United States of America

First Printing — January 2015

Contents

Introduction
to Growing a
Strong Marriage

Welcome to Growing a Strong Marriage! Over the next few weeks we hope to strengthen and challenge you in your marriage as you go on this journey together with the other couples in your Bible study group.

This study on marriage is a unique one. You have been invited to hear stories from people who you probably already know and respect. Perhaps you have read their books, and now you have the opportunity to hear directly from them and their spouses on one of the most important aspects of their lives: marriage. Marriage has its difficulties and its joys. As two people journey through life together, they experience many different circumstances and learn more about each other and themselves. Whether you have been married for a few years or thirty years, there is always more to learn about each other and room to grow as a couple.

What is this series about? It is about creating an opportunity for you to grow a strong marriage so that when life's distractions and difficulties come your way, you will be rooted together in Christ and confident that you both are committed to making this marriage work. Through the videos, discussion with fellow couples in your group, and Bible study, we hope that truth will penetrate your marriage and provide nutrients that continue to enrich growth far beyond these next few weeks.

Know that this series is not a quick fix that will make all your marriage troubles go away. Rather it is a starting point for deeper communication and understanding with each other. No one ever said marriage would be easy, but it is certainly worth the effort. Also know that this series is not meant to be a solution to serious crises that sometime find their way into a marriage, such as adultery, violence, or addiction, to name a few. If you are facing any of these more serious issues, it is strongly encouraged that you seek good marriage counseling to help you work through them. If you need recommendations, your pastor can provide referral options. It is best if both attend counseling.

The Growing a Strong Marriage series is divided into three sections. The first study guide covers the biblical foundations of marriage. The second study guide addresses communication and conflict and has a bonus session on remarriage. The third and final study guide covers children, unexpected challenges, and staying connected, and has a bonus session on adoption. The sessions and study guides can be used individually or out of order, but it is recommended that they be completed in the order they are presented.

Over these next few weeks, we will learn from couples such John and Stasi Eldredge, Gary and Lisa Thomas, and Art and Lysa TerKeurst on how they handle conflict, communication, and life's difficulties. Chip and Theresa Ingram, Gordon and Gail MacDonald, and Les and Leslie Parrott will also join the conversation on topics such as the purpose of marriage, kids, and having fun together. Join them now in their living rooms, grab a cup of coffee, and listen to the stories and insights they have to share.

Introduction to Working Together

Although each marriage is unique, there are many aspects common to every marriage. Every marriage is made of two people with different backgrounds and different expectations. Every marriage has troubles of its own. Every marriage has room to grow stronger in two important areas: communication and resolving conflict.

The first two sessions in this volume of Growing a Strong Marriage address the cornerstone of marriage that we call "communication." Healthy communication is essential for a strong, growing relationship. It not only provides ways for us to get to know each other more fully, but it also helps us to keep from falling into deep conflict and aids us to climb out together when we do. The first of these two sessions will focus on communication and what the Bible has to say about it. The second session will dive into some helpful communication tools and suggestions for growing in this area together.

In the third session of this study we will look at conflict itself. As married Christians, how should we approach conflict? Is conflict normal? What do we do when we just can't seem to reach a resolution? We will look at these questions as well as the values of commitment to each another and giving grace and forgiveness

As you can see, these are essential topics and issues for every marriage. So let's begin and see what the couples in the video have to share from their own wisdom, insight, and experience.

Communication 1— Talking Together

There is one whose rash words are like sword thrusts, but the tongue of the wise brings healing. —Proverbs 12:18

Watch Session #1 now.

How often have you seen a sitcom in which there is some sort of misunderstanding? Assumptions, jumping to conclusions, hearing skewed information through the grapevine—it's often there. It's always funny and always cleared up by the end. But why is it funny, and how does this plot line continue to entertain audiences time and time again? Because we can so easily relate. Miscommunication happens—a lot. Sometimes it's harmless. Sometimes it's humorous. But other times miscommunication or lack of communication can do serious harm to a relationship. After all, communication is how we relate to each other, verbally and nonverbally. When that connection is damaged, twisted, or cut off, many other problems will naturally follow.

Do you remember a recent situation of poor communication that turned funny in your life, whether with your spouse or someone else? Share it with the group. (If the circumstance is with your spouse, agree together to share before you do so.)

Communication and the Bible

Healthy communication is a critical aspect of every marriage and the Bible is not silent on this issue. Proverbs especially shares a great deal of wisdom and instruction on life, relationships, and pleasing the Lord. Read through the following verses together, and then discuss and write down what each has to say on communication, the good and the bad.

Proverbs 12:18

Proverbs 15:1

Proverbs 17:4

A few different insights about what we say and how we say it may have jumped out to you. First of all, we can see in these verses that our words produce a consequence and have a profound effect on the conversation, the outcome, and the other person. Rash and harsh words stir up anger, which is not a pretty picture. Not only does the conversation become more heated and move further away from a peaceful resolution, but words can deeply hurt one another. These pains are not simple surface wounds; they go deep inside like the excruciating thrust of a sword.

The words we say to each other are powerful. They can be damaging, but they can also bring healing. "The tongue of the wise brings healing" and a "soft answer turns away wrath." What a drastically different picture! Instead of deep, lasting pain, these types of words bring healing, nourishment, and peace. Rather than the conversation escalating and being fueled with more anger, these words turn away wrath. Fueled reaction is replaced by gentleness and understanding.

Imagine you and your spouse just had a disagreement and you begin to talk about it. Imagine your conversation consisted of the first scenario with the rash and harsh words. What is the result? Would you both be satisfied? What are you doing afterward?

Now imagine you and your spouse had the same disagreement, but your conversation happened within this second scenario of wisdom and soft answers. What is the result of this conversation? Would you both be satisfied? How different does it make you feel? What are you doing afterward?

You probably prefer the second scenario. It naturally produces a happier ending and will strengthen the marriage relationship rather than bruise it. But which one is easier and more natural to do? Probably the first. It works out of our reactions, our desire to be heard, and our pride.

However, the second scenario is certainly possible. Moving in this direction is what will help you grow a stronger marriage. The key here is this: You have a choice. You are not a victim of your reactions. You have the choice of whether you are going to use your words to bring pain or healing. You have the choice of whether you are going to pour words of anger or peace into the conversation. Proverbs 17:14 reflects the wisdom that can be found in this choice: "The beginning of strife is like letting out water, so quit before the quarrel breaks out." You have a choice. Communicate well. Choose understanding and choose to quit strife before a bigger problem erupts. What choice are you going to make?

Let's summarize our first lesson in this way: *Choose words that bring healing.*

Let's take a look at another set of proverbs. Read through the following verses in the same way and take note of what each one has to say about communication. Can you detect a theme?

Proverbs 18:2

Proverbs 18:13

Proverbs 18:17

Proverbs 29:20

What do these verses have in common? They all talk about the *fool*, right? All throughout Proverbs the foolish person and wise person are contrasted. They each live very different lives and make very different decisions. The book of Proverbs repeatedly encourages the reader to choose wisdom and obedience to the Lord over foolishness, whims, and self-centeredness, especially when this dangerous path appears easier and more enticing.

These verses you just read paint a picture of the foolish person in how he communicates with others. The fool takes no pleasure in understanding, but only in expressing his own opinion. Think about this person for a moment. Imagine there is a problem that needs to be solved or an idea that you want to communicate, but this person's reaction is only to launch into something that relates to him. You try to get a word in about what you're really trying to say, but he is not interested in understanding. He just wants to be sure that he shares his opinion and that you hear it.

But before we become too judgmental here, we need to ask ourselves how often we "assume" something. How often do you hear one word and immediately think you know what your spouse is trying to say? How often do you assume where something is going, close your ears, and open your mouth? Although this is foolishness, we all do it—at least occasionally. But remember that the fool takes no pleasure in understanding. He only wants to make his point.

The fool is also hasty in his words. He gives an answer before he hears the question or has all the information. He seems perfectly correct in all he says, without a doubt— until someone else says something, that is. Have you ever had a really good point you wanted to make, you made it, and then someone else pointed out a piece of information you were not aware of that then negates your entire opinion? The fault here is not in having a constructive conversation, but in having an attitude of arrogance in thinking you are completely right and no one else's opinion could possibly matter. The fool speaks quickly and is unwilling to listen to the thoughts, ideas, and opinions of others.

If these are characteristics of the fool, the opposite is true of the wise. Who is the wise person? The wise person takes pleasure in understanding and is more concerned about truth and understanding than in expressing his own opinion. The wise person listens patiently and allows others to talk first, knowing he could look foolish if he answers before he has all the facts. The wise person is humble and has self-control. There is great hope for this person.

The second lesson have learned here is: *Desire understanding over having your own voice heard.*

Now read these next few verses from Proverbs, taking note of the comparisons that are made.

Proverbs 12:15

Proverbs 15:28

Proverbs 15:31

Proverbs 29:11

In this set of verses, the wise person is compared directly with the fool. The fool vents out everything he has to say. It's a verbal explosion that can't be stopped, which certainly does not allow for meaningful dialogue. The wise person, however, thinks before he speaks and holds back his reaction in self-constraint. Again, the point here is not to go to such an extreme that you don't express anything, but that you not give "full vent to your spirit." Think first, and then respond. Visceral reactions can be dangerous, especially if they are based on hasty assumptions. The key is to practice wisdom in communication. Listen and think about your response rather than blurting out the first thought. Such venting leads to hurt feelings and regret rather than to resolution.

Lastly, we are left with a picture of the wise person. The wise person listens to advice and life-giving reproof. Even when the truth hurts, the wise person listens, grows, and moves on. Increasing in healthy communication is an area in which we all can improve. Choose wisdom. Choose to listen and establish fair ground where each of you has the invitation to talk. Make your first priority to understand your spouse and his or her point, rather than making your own. Take pleasure in understanding each other.

The lesson we learned here is: *Be wise in your reactions and listen carefully.*

This is the final proverb we will look at today. What wisdom does it share?

Proverbs 26:18–19

This last verse highlights the importance of honesty and truthfulness in your communication with each other. Some may struggle with this more than others. We know it is unfair to say something hurtful or spiteful to a spouse— something you really meant at the time, whether intentionally or impulsively—and then try to brush it off by saying that you were only joking. Saying it was a joke does not negate that it was said, and actually probably does reflect a true feeling in you that your spouse may recognize. Put off deceitful speech, be honest, and own up to hurtful things you say and ask forgiveness.

The University of Relationships

Life gets busy. Many demands call to us from all different directions throughout the day. It's a wonder sometimes that we even see our spouse, let alone manage to work in a worthwhile conversation. Yet talking with each other is incredibly important. Elsewhere the TerKeursts share that they sometimes feel like "two ships passing in the night." It's so easy to fall into the busyness of life that we may take each other, our marriage, and our quality conversation for granted. But for the sake of your marriage, talk! Find a way—it's that crucial.

Make time to talk with each other without kids or other distractions. This will likely look different in various seasons of life and that's perfectly okay. What is called "quality conversation" when newly married will look different from a "quality conversation" when two children have come along and are demanding all your attention. The important thing is to get that time in. However you can make it happen, just do it.

"[The marriage conference] gave us a language to talk about fears, wounds, history, and family." —John Eldredge

As psychologists, the Parrotts have extensive experience in helping couples improve their communication. This is because marriage problems often come back to just that. We all have different expectations, which counter each other and cause problems. We can only get through them by talking. Let's take a look at some of the areas that were touched on in the video.

Family of Origin

According to the Parrots, everyone is trained in a "University of Relationships." The main classes of the university are usually led by the family in which you grew up. Other classes are led by your culture, your church, your friends, and the media. The lessons we learn in this university vary for each person. Some lessons you will want to mirror. Some lessons you will react against and never want to follow. Many lessons rub off on you, and you never even knew it happened.

"When you become aware of how that family that you came from shaped you, you'll have a lot more power in how this relationship gets formed between the two of you." —Les Parrott

In what way have you noticed that your University of Relationships has affected your marriage?

Les and Leslie named a few of the lessons: what it means to be on time, how to celebrate a birthday, how to feel loved, how to handle money, what married life looks like, and how to manage the social calendar.

In which of these classes were you and your spouse taught different lessons? What other lessons from the University of Relationships would you add?

Talk with each other about the differences of your universities as they arise day to day. Many of these lessons are exposed when a couple is dating and first married, but more of them are exposed through the years as new seasons of life come and go. Simply recognizing these lessons and saying them out loud can bring clarity to a situation. The awareness of how they shaped you informs what you become, whether the same or different.

We learn many lessons from the various influences in our lives. Let's look at a few of these in a little more detail.

Roles

Just because you were raised a certain way does not mean that's the way it has to be in your family with your spouse. Your spouse had a different experience and has different ideas. Neither one of you can duplicate your family of origin to your family now. Instead, you need to work together to decide and define what both of you want your family to be. You get to make your own decisions together to create your own identity. This isn't your family or your spouse's family. This is your family together.

Children

Strict or lenient? Equal effort or mainly the responsibility of one? Who takes care of discipline? Are the kids involved in extracurricular activities? Who is picking them up from where and when? Although children and marriage will be covered in more detail in a later session, it's important to address that this is a big area in which you are likely going to have different experiences and opinions. Your own childhood is going to affect what you have to say. Talk through your picture of raising your children before they come and then as they grow up.

Finances

At the end of the video, Gordon and Gail MacDonald shared the importance they found in being on the same page concerning finances. Money fights and money problems are sore spots in many marriages. Although this is not the space to go into a detailed study on money, it is a place to discuss the importance of talking about money.

> *"[Financial] conflicts erode every other dimension of your relationship. Not just money, but it begins to infect every other area of living together."* —Gordon MacDonald

Similar to all other areas of marriage, husband and wife have different histories with money and come from families that deal with money in different ways. Gordon and Gail came from different homes and have different attitudes toward finances, but they were able to come together and make their own plans, priorities, and ways of doing things.

The MacDonalds' financial plan is to:

- Live debt free
- Give a minimum of a tithe
- Send kids to college debt free
- Responsibly put money away for later years

What are your thoughts concerning these goals? What might you add?

Whatever your financial plans, it's important to have plans together and be in agreement on them. Sit down together once a month and talk about what you are going to do for the month. Make decisions together and stick to them. A sure way to damage trust in a marriage is to spend money in a way that upsets, disappoints, or scares one's spouse. A great way to strengthen trust, however, is for each other to be fully informed of what is going to happen so that there aren't any surprises. Stable spending and saving can bring a great sense of security to a marriage. Plus, sitting down and deciding together where your money goes will, over time, enhance your unity as you work together on such important issues.

Which of these areas (roles, children, finances, and so on) are stronger areas for you and your spouse to discuss and gain common ground on? Which ones are more difficult?

It's normal to butt heads and have differences on these topics, especially early in marriage. Like the Parrotts said, every person has a different University of Relationships. So if it's normal and natural for you to have differences, it should also be expected and necessary to talk out those differences. Explain to each other what you expect, understand what each other is saying, and decide together where you can find a compromise.

Study Each Other and Have Fun

Communication is not just about fixing problems. It is also about being together, enjoying each other, and developing your relationship. Talk regularly about your day, your concerns, your fears, your dreams, and the world around you.

"In those moments, if you can laugh about it instead of cry about it, it shifts the tone of the relationship." —Leslie Parrott

Les and Leslie suggested that this process of communication should be approached with objectivity and a sense of humor. Objectivity forces you to step out of your own feelings and expectations and figure out why you are acting or thinking a certain way. In this way, you can best understand yourself and explain your thoughts and feelings to your spouse. A sense of humor is essential because often we pick up habits and expectations we didn't even know we had. Find the humor in them and laugh together at how different your "universities" really were.

Questions for Home

What are some areas in communication that are good growing opportunities for you as individuals and as a couple?

Did one of the verses in Proverbs especially stand out to you? If so, why?

Set aside a time this week to talk together without distractions.

What are your financial goals? How do you plan to get there? Look at your finances realistically together, make a plan together, work together, and dream together.

Communication 2— Listening Well

Let no corrupting talk come out of your mouths, but only such as is good for building up, as fits the occasion, that it may give grace to those who hear. (Ephesians 4:29)

Watch Session #2 now (pause when indicated on the video).

In the last session we talked about the importance of communicating and communicating well. But how do we get there? In this session we are going to look at tools you can use to grow strong together in the way you communicate, one step at a time. But first, let's take a look at a few first-things-first items.

Time and Commitment

Stronger communication is not going to happen overnight. In fact, the times your communication skills are tested and have the best opportunity to grow is exactly when those difficult moments come. Your efficiency and clarity of communication with each other will improve as you commit to each other to establish new ways of relating to each other and make the conscious decision to break out of old habits that don't work.

Trust

Art and Lysa shared that they had to develop growing levels of trust with each other in order to build better communication. For example, when Art brought Lysa the Diet Coke, she reacted out of her own insecurities but then realized what was happening. She trusted Art that he was not out to hurt her and that he did not think the same way about her as she thought about herself. She trusts him and knows that she can be honest and vulnerable about how she really feels. Such trust takes time to grow. However, this type of trust within communication is a circular growth. In a healthy marriage, the more you trust, the more you will feel you can share. Then the more you share, the more intimate the relationship becomes and the more you will trust. As Stasi Eldredge said previously, sometimes she knew she needed to share and open up with John even when she didn't *feel* at the time that it was safe to share. Yet she *knew* she could trust him and decided to open up and be honest anyway.

Give Grace

As you work through this process and grow stronger together, give each other grace. Sometimes we don't always say something exactly how we want to say it. Certain feelings and concerns are difficult to put into words. Allow each other time to express yourselves and try not to latch onto a certain phrase, especially if it wasn't what the other person really meant. Give your spouse the benefit of the doubt. You would want the same grace to be shown to you. Also, in a healthy marriage your spouse isn't saying something to *want* to hurt you. If one does say something that truly is hurtful, then forgiveness should be sought. In the same way, Art meant nothing hurtful by accidentally getting Lysa a Diet Coke, and Lysa gave him grace, knowing he didn't intend the message she felt.

Don't Hoard Retaliation Rocks

In the video Lysa talked about what she refers to as "retaliation rocks." These rocks start to pile up over time when we don't talk about what is bothering us. Instead, either through a noble attempt to keep peace or intentionally being passive aggressive, we stuff problems down and hold feelings in. But those rocks don't just sit in a neatly stacked pile forever. One day, the rock pile becomes too heavy and they have to go somewhere. The tipping point occurs and all former grievances come flying, making this one problem far larger and more hurtful than it has to be. Rocks hurt.

Instead of hoarding retaliation rocks, make it a point not to collect them. When something is wrong, talk about it. Rather than stuff it down only to explode later, talk about it together and let it be resolved.

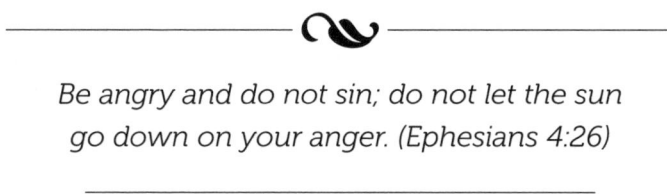

Be angry and do not sin; do not let the sun go down on your anger. (Ephesians 4:26)

This verse is a great rule of thumb and often shared at Christian weddings. Resolve your differences in love and grace. Be careful not to let them carry over into another day. As Gail MacDonald says elsewhere, it is important to keep short accounts with each other. Resolution and forgiveness lead to true peace in a relationship, not ignoring the problem.

Commit to Kindness

Read Ephesians 4:17–32.

Let's take a look at this passage step-by-step.

Off with the Old, On with the New (4:17–24)

In this passage Paul reminds the believers in Ephesus that in Christ their lives have changed. The way he explains this is through the old self and the new self. The old self is characterized by sin, alienation from God, hard hearts, greed, and impurity. As Christians, however, this is no longer how we live. There has been a radical change in Christ! The new self reflects God and is righteous and holy. We cannot live from both the old and the new. One of them has to go. In this manner, Paul is urging the church in Ephesus to live out of this new self in their relationships with others and in every other area of life.

As Christians, this most undoubtedly applies to marriage, which is the most intimate relationship we have. In the remaining verses of this passage, Paul lays out this difference even more clearly and gives specific examples of the new self in real life.

The New Self in Real Life (4:25–32)

Take a look at Ephesians 4:25–28. Write out the characteristics of the old self and the new self.

Old Self	New Self
ignorance *anger* *rage*	

How then is this expressed in marriage? By letting your marriage be characterized by truth. Be honest with each other in all things and reflect the truth that is in Christ. Even when you are upset or frustrated, do not sin. One may ask, "How is it possible to be angry and not sin?" There is nothing wrong with being angry; what matters is what you do out of that anger. You have a choice. Be careful not to give the devil a foothold in your marriage. As John and Stasi Eldredge said elsewhere, the devil seeks to destroy all that is good, including your marriage. Be careful that the door is not opened to destructive thoughts, attitudes, or actions toward each other.

Read Ephesians 4:29 and fill out the box in the same way.

Old Self	New Self

This is the verse that Lysa mentioned, which should be committed to memory to serve as a reminder when you may be tempted to speak unkind words. In Christ, your new self only speaks that which builds up your spouse. Gone are the days of words that intentionally brought hurt. Such words were not only harmful to your marriage, but were poison to your spouse's soul. Instead, speak to your spouse words that bring grace, that which is freely given. Discover what will lift up your spouse and offer words of strength and encouragement. Express what you love about your spouse. To some, such encouragement may come naturally. But if you happen to be someone who doesn't think naturally in this way, when you do it will speak even louder. Speak words of grace and encouragement to your spouse this week.

Lastly, let's take a look at Ephesians 4:30–32. You know what to do.

Old Self	New Self

Here we have a list of more characteristics of the old self that should be put off. Maybe in your heart one of these has taken hold. If so, for the sake of your own soul and your marriage, put off the bitterness, anger, slander, or malice that holds you down. How do you get there? It's not going to be an instantaneous change but a process of renewal by the Holy Spirit. It starts with what Paul mentions at the end of this passage: forgiveness.

No marriage and no person are perfect. As much as you may desire to put off all corrupt speech, you will still slip and hurt your spouse on occasion. You will also be hurt. When this does happen, "Forgive one another as God in Christ forgave you." If you don't, you are setting yourself up for bitterness, anger, slander, and retaliation rocks. That is what the old self would have done. But you no longer live in the old self. In Christ, you live in the new self, and in him you can commit yourself to kindness, be tenderhearted, and forgive each other.

How does this application of looking at the old self and the new self within your marriage affect what you think about yourself, your spouse, and your relationship?

Tools

Tools are not magical. A hammer on its own cannot build a house, but in the hands of someone who uses it a beautiful home can happen. In the same way, simply knowing about these communication tools is not going to turn your world around. They will have their desired effect only as you use them and practice with them. Let's take a look at some of the tools Art and Lysa shared with us in the video that they use in their own marriage.

Tool 1: "This Is What I'm Thinking. Now Tell Me What You Meant."

Thinking back to the Diet Coke story, is there any part you can relate to? If so, in what way?

When Art walked in with the Diet Coke, Lysa reacted. She was upset and hurt and couldn't believe he would do that to her. But she then realized that things weren't quite matching up. She knew Art would not intentionally hurt her. So she interrupted the moment by saying, "This is what I'm thinking. Now tell me what you meant."

"Every couple is going to bring [unrealistic and realistic expectations] into the marriage, and you've got to focus on communicating those and then creatively meet what those realistic expectations are." —Art TerKeurst

This is a good example of being objective in the midst of a contentious moment. She was able to have the awareness that what she was feeling might not be what was happening. Sure enough, once she was able to take a breath, express what she thought was going on, and allow him to explain his side, the problem dissipated. She was able to see that he wasn't trying to give her a hint that she needed a *Diet* Coke; it was an honest mistake. Problem solved.

How easy it is to read too much into things at times! As you practice awareness and objectivity in your communication with your spouse, you will be able to spot the times when you need to say, "Okay, this is what I'm thinking. Now tell me what you meant." Laying it all on the table helps to clear up any miscommunication that may be happening and bring you onto the same page.

Tool 2: The Three Questions

Disagreements and arguments will always happen. Emotions of frustration and even anger can get pumping. This tool brings us back to two points in Ephesians that we discussed: "In your anger do not sin" and "Let no corrupting talk come out of your mouths." In these heated discussions, ask yourself the following three questions:

1. Are my words kind?

2. Are my words necessary?

3. Are my words true?

And be careful not to twist the intention of these questions. As Lysa shared, working with these questions is really hard. Especially in the moment, it's easy to think that your words are "necessary" to get your point across or that these words are "true for me!" But there is a larger purpose in mind. Are the words showing kindness toward your spouse? Are the words necessary for the resolution of the problem so that you can work together? Are the words true statements, or am I twisting or being dramatic with my words? This tool, along with others, requires a great deal of self-control and practice, but it will transform how you talk with each other.

"Am I trying to prove that I am right or am I trying to improve the relationship? If I am trying to prove that I am right, it is going to lead to conflict escalation instead of conflict dissipation." —Lysa TerKeurst

Tool 3: The Three-Second Pause

This tool is similar to the three-questions tool in that it requires you to be self-controlled and push the pause button. Rather than letting arguments roll on out of control, take a three-second pause before you respond. This will allow you to keep from saying what you might later regret. It also allows you a moment to think and ask yourself the three questions.

More importantly, the three-second pause allows emotions to briefly settle and you can instead allow the Holy Spirit to intervene, as Art and Lysa mentioned. Let him be the mediator and allow him to work on your hearts and bring love, peace, understanding, and grace into the conversation.

Tool 4: Active Listening

In the video Art shared a story about his buddy listening to his wife's story about her terrible experience with the broken shopping cart.

What did the women in your group think about this story? Does this kind of listening, done in a genuine manner, matter to you?

What did the men in your group think about this story? Did it make sense to you?

The shopping cart story is humorous, but it makes a big point. For most women this type of active listening matters a great deal and speaks volumes. Although Art's friend might have felt that he was exaggerating and being a little over the top as he was responding to his wife, to her it meant a lot and she loved it.

Active listening may seem strange to some, but to others it is a strong symbol of love and affirmation. What is active listening exactly? Active listening goes beyond just hearing what is said. Rather than the occasional "Oh—uh huh— yup" in response, the listener shows he or she is actively taking in what is being said. The key to active listening is reflecting back on what is heard. For example, in the shopping cart story if the husband would have simply been listening, she may have told a brief story of her troubles, and the husband might have responded with either a single syllable response or even a "that's annoying." But instead he chose to actively listen to her and respond throughout the story with comments such as, "You mean the cart with the bumpy wheel . . . the one that just can't move right? . . . Oh, that had to be so annoying! . . . I know, I've had that before too! . . . I'm amazed you put up with it the whole time!"

These types of responses showed her that he was not only really listening to her but that he was engaged and cared about her and her experience.

Another way to listen well is to really listen. This may seem obvious, but it is worth discussing. We talked previously about how tempting it is to assume what someone is talking about, and then respond to that assumption rather than waiting to see what the person really has to say. Related to this is the temptation to interrupt. Some personalities have a tendency to interrupt what someone else is saying in order perhaps to help complete a thought, to show agreement, or maybe to hurry the conversation along. If you have a tendency to do this (and especially if it is something you already know annoys your spouse), give the gift of listening to complete thoughts. Don't jump in to complete the sentence or add new ideas, but instead just listen intently. Be patient and allow your spouse to get out all he or she wants to say.

Tool 5: Conferences

If you paused the video where it prompted, you haven't seen the last tool quite yet. We'll return to the video in a just a moment, but let's first talk about what you're going to see. For this final portion, you will see Chip and Theresa Ingram give an example of a tool that has been valuable in their marriage. When they went to marriage counseling together, their counselor told them they needed to improve their communication and suggested they have regular "conferences." At first they had these conferences daily, but as their marriage strengthened they were able to have them less often, though they still keep them up even to this day, sitting down to their conferences at least once a week.

The conferences have specific rules:

- Each person takes turn asking the other person three specific questions. The first asks the question, the second responds. When the second is done answering the question, he or she asks the same question to the first. When the first is done answering the question, he or she then moves on to the next question and the process continues from there.

- When it is your turn to ask the question, you are only allowed to listen. At no point are you to offer solutions or suggestions, or discuss an issue in any way. Metaphorical duct tape has been placed over your mouth. This is an exercise in listening and allowing each other to share freely. When it is your turn to answer the question, then you have the freedom to give your personal answers without interruption.

- The three questions are:

  1. What are you concerned about?

  2. What do you wish?

  3. What are you willing to do?

Chip and Theresa have kindly modeled for us what a conference looks like. They have kept many comments general in front of the camera, as they are referring their own personal situations. However, when you are with your spouse in the privacy of your own home, be as detailed and honest with each other as you can.

Return now to the video and resume watching.

What is your reaction to this conferencing tool?

You are now well on your way to improving your communication and growing a stronger marriage! Strengthening your marriage is an ongoing process. Be encouraged that the more you put into improving this foundational area, the stronger your marriage will be.

Questions for Home

Which communication tool stood out to you the most? In what way do you plan to implement the tool this week?

Carve out some time within the next couple days to sit down and have a conference together. Take it beyond "We should do that" to "This is when we are going to do that." Decide now, together, when will be best and write it down here.

Challenge each other to memorize Ephesians 4:29. The one who truly commits it to memory first, gets a special treat. You decide.

When Conflict Grows and Remains

Do nothing from selfish ambition or conceit,
but in humility count others more significant
than yourselves. (Philippians 2:3)

Watch Session #3 now.

At this point, you might be starting to feel that you are really getting to know these couples in the videos. Their honesty and, at times, silliness might make you feel like they are sitting right there with you.

Many would probably agree that it is in the video for this session that they have been the most open and vulnerable. It's one thing to give some good advice and offer wisdom on how to have a strong marriage. It's an entirely new level to share with you the nature of the real struggles and strained seasons of marriage these couples have been through.

What are some themes or insights that stood out to you in the video?

Each marriage is different, but every marriage will have troubles of some kind. Challenges come in seasons and you can take these as "growth opportunities," as the TerKeursts called them. Some couples have a really tough time in their first years of marriage, whereas for others it's a relatively smooth transition. For some, new challenges that strain the marriage come along with having children or at about the seven-year anniversary. As the Eldredges shared, having children suddenly takes away much of the time you used to have together, and easily leads to distance and loneliness if you don't take proactive steps toward each other.

If you've ever wondered if there is a perfect marriage out there, hopefully today you've heard a resounding No! There is no perfect marriage. Even the husband and wife, who are both psychologists and have written countless books on marriage and make a living helping people with marriage, got in a fight on their way to a seminar they were teaching on marriage and conflict! There is no perfect marriage, but there certainly are *great* marriages. This session centers on one of those turning points that can really make a marriage great: what you do with conflict.

Let's look at conflict from two different angles—when conflict is still fresh, and when conflict has remained present for some time.

When Conflict Arises

Have you ever gone out to your car and noticed that a tire looked a little low? It's nothing too serious, definitely not flat. Maybe you are even able to drive on it all day with no problems. But just to be safe, you stop by an air pump on the way home and fill it up. Now you're good to go! Then a week or so goes by and you again notice the tire is a little low. You top it off with some air and continue on your way. You're busy and don't really have time to sit at the garage to try to get it fixed, and they might not be able to find the problem anyway. You continue this process for a couple months, occasionally topping it off to get you through the next few days. Then that one fateful morning, you are running late and find, yes, a completely flat tire. Turns out there was a small nail in the tire. The mechanic tells you that if you had taken care of it when it was first a problem, it would have been an easy removal and patch. But over time, the problem became worse, causing far bigger problems.

This is how it is sometimes with "smaller" conflicts—when things are stuffed under the rug because we just don't want to deal with them. When conflict does arise between you and your spouse, you should deal with it from the beginning so it doesn't become a larger problem later. The longer it sits the bigger and more damaging it becomes.

Fight Well

Les and Leslie have a book all about conflict called *The Good Fight: How Conflict Can Bring You Closer* (Worthy, 2013). In it they talk about the difference between a good fight and a bad fight. Conflicts and fights are going to happen, but how are you going to approach them? Take a look at the differences.

	Bad Fight	Good Fight
Goal	Winning the fight	Resolving the fight
Topic	Surface issues	Underlying issues
Emphasis	Personalities and power struggles	Ideas and issues
Attitude	Confrontational and defensive	Cooperative and receptive
Motivation	Shift blame	Take responsibility
Mode	Belittle	Respect
Manner	Egocentric	Empathetic
Demeanor	Self-righteous	Understanding
Side Effect	Escalation of tension	Easing of tension
Result	Discord	Harmony
Benefit	Stagnation and distance	Growth and intimacy

What are your observations or responses to this chart?

If you could summarize each type of fight in one word, what would it be?

Someone may have suggested "Destructive vs. Healthy." Another may have said "Nonproductive vs. Productive." Someone else may have stated the obvious by saying "Bad vs. Good." What about "Pride vs. Humility"? This is the main point the Parrotts make in their book. Bad fights center on pride. Take another look through the lists. Doesn't the "Bad Fight" reek of pride and the "Good Fight" savor of humility?

Pride does not lead to a stronger marriage. In fact, Scripture has a good deal to say about pride. Take a look at the following verses and write down what you learn about pride:

Proverbs 16:18

Proverbs 29:23

Philippians 2:3–4

Everyone struggles with pride, so how then do we work against that pride and grow in humility? Such humility in the midst of conflict requires a significant attitude adjustment and heart change. Most importantly, you need to pray for your own heart and attitude. This deep change can be removed and replaced only by the work of the Holy Spirit in your life. Pray also for your spouse, that your marriage would be characterized by humility and mutual submission to one another (Ephesians 5:18). Pray that the Holy Spirit would continually renew your minds to see clearly, live humbly, and love each other as Christ loves the church.

Remember this: If pride is an excessive focus on yourself, your desires, and your needs, then humility is putting aside your own self and thinking of your spouse first. Make it a point to have empathy; that is, try to see your spouse's perspective. Taking this one intentional step will make a great difference in how you handle conflict.

When you fight, have a *good* fight, and you will actually grow closer rather than apart.

The Mercy-Centered Relationship

In the video, Gordon and Gail MacDonald talked about repentance and forgiveness. How would you explain the importance of repentance and forgiveness in marriage?

According to Gordon, this is what distinctly qualifies as a Christian relationship: a mercy-centered relationship. Mercy is withholding what is otherwise deserved, and grace is freely giving what has not been deserved. As children of God, we have been given both by our heavenly Father. We know what it means to be utterly sinful, deserving of death. But instead of judgment, he gives us eternal life through the sacrifice of his Son. Because as Christians we have been shown such mercy and grace, we should also show the same to our spouse. Forgiveness is a powerful gift.

"To the extent that [repentance or forgiveness] misses in a relationship, the whole thing falls apart." —Gordon MacDonald

Both repentance and forgiveness are absolutely necessary in a strong marriage. Over the course of your marriage you will have many opportunities to practice both. Practice this even in the small offenses. Let's take a look at them separately.

Repentance

Repentance is important because you are acknowledging you have messed up. This is more than asking for forgiveness. Repentance is a direct acknowledgement of what you have done wrong, which again requires sincere humility. As Gordon explained, repentance is also a confession of one's rebellious spirit and a commitment to learn and grow from this experience and endeavor not to repeat it. Repentance and confession allow space for trust to begin to build again. But depending on the degree of the offense, it may take time for trust to be built up again, even after you have been forgiven.

Forgiveness

It is not enough for the wrongdoer to repent; it is then the offended person's place to extend forgiveness when he or she is ready. Forgiveness is a complex and, at times, complicated matter, especially for more serious issues. Forgiveness is not a happy fuzzy feeling. It is a decision to no longer hold something against another person. You no longer harbor it against the other and are not storing it up to be ammunition in a future conversation.

Just because you have forgiven your spouse does not mean everything will automatically be back to the way things were before. Depending on what happened, trust may need to be built back up, which can take time. Repentance and forgiveness do not automatically heal relationships, but they are essential first steps in that direction.

"All the times whenever we hurt each other, we have to decide—are we going to center on one thing done wrong, or are we going to take the many years of doing things right and well?" —Gail MacDonald

There Is No Back Door

Most people don't go into marriage expecting it to end. Yet sadly many marriages do end. *Divorce* has become a common word tossed around, whereas not even a century ago it was nearly unheard of in daily culture. Although there are real and serious reasons for divorce (such as unfaithfulness or abuse), it should not be an alternative to doing the hard work of working out challenging marriage issues. The TerKeursts hit days when they really didn't feel like being married anymore. The Eldredges had the idea of divorce on the table more than once, but they are still together.

Here's a refresher of their advice in the video:

> *There is no back door. . . . Divorce is not an option. We're going in and we're not going out.*
> —Lisa Thomas

> *You've got to do whatever you can do to make marriage work . . . even if it means losing your job, friends. . . . Divorce is not even an option. It's not even a word on the table. We have to do what we have to do in order to knit this marriage into the oneness that God intended it to be. —Art TerKeurst*

> *The grass isn't going to be greener on the other side. The grass is greener where you water and fertilize it. I had to start watering and fertilizing my marriage.*
> —Lysa TerKeurst

The best thing we ever did was get counseling. . . .
We knew the healthier you are, the healthier I am, the
healthier the marriage is going to be. . . . We are big
believers in getting your story in front of someone else.
   —John Eldredge

We knew there was more available—and there is! It's
worth fighting for. You can have a good marriage, a
friendship, a companionship . . . a shared life together.
   —John and Stasi Eldredge

A turning point in our marriage [was that] we went to
counseling and it was worth it. . . . [The counselor] took
me to the Word, and he taught me how to take those
negative thoughts and replace them with Scripture.
   —Theresa Ingram

Reflect on this advice. Does one of these stand out to you in an
influential way? If so, which one and in what way? Share this
with your group.

A good, strong marriage doesn't just happen. It must be worked on and invested into—though this is much easier said than done. Keep that commitment to each other that you are not going anywhere and that you are in this for the long haul. Have the attitude that Gary and Lisa Thomas talked about that "there is no back door." The option of ending marriage is not even "on the table." Like them, work through your tough seasons, no matter what it takes. Keep this commitment so sacred that you never even joke about it being otherwise. For example, stay away from threatening divorce for the sake of argument or just to get someone's attention—this would be an example of a "bad fight" and unfair tactics.

"The grass isn't greener on the other side.
The grass is greener where you water
and fertilize it." —Lysa TerKeurst

One day, Art and Lysa sat across from their pastor and were told that without the intervention of God in their lives, there was no hope for their marriage. What a wake-up call! Wisely, they did allow God to intervene in their lives and have grown individually and together as a result. The truth is, though, that all of our marriages need God's intervention. It's a wonder any marriage makes it. Allow God to intervene regularly in your own marriage.

In another circumstance, Art's father told him that, no matter what, he needed to make his marriage work. Even if it meant sacrificing his job, hobbies, or friends, his wife came first. Yet sometimes we sacrifice our marriage in order to pursue a job, a hobby, or friends, thinking that our spouse will "understand." If there are real problems with your marriage, it's time to switch your priorities. Your job, hobbies, and friends are all good things, and spouses certainly can and should give room for us to enjoy these things. However, they are *never* more important than your spouse. Your spouse comes first; let this be evident in what you say, how you spend your time, and in the regular life decisions you make.

When Conflict Grows and Remains

How then do we keep this unconditional commitment to each other when those especially dark, frustrating seasons in marriage arrive? Thinking back to the video, what do you remember were the turning points in the lives of these couples?

Let's take a look at some of the themes they shared with us.

The Objective Mirror

One of the most resounding themes in this video was that so many of the couples went to counseling. Were you surprised to hear this? What are your thoughts about marriage counseling?

Some couples are afraid of the idea of going to counseling or think that it would never be for them. "Marriage counseling is only for people with real problems. We can get through this on our own," they might say. However, counseling is not only for "severe cases." As the Eldredges shared, there wasn't any violence. They weren't throwing things or yelling at each other. They were just lonely, distant, and had lost the closeness they used to feel. Counseling is not only an okay idea, it's a great idea!

The objectivity of a counselor can be used to look into yourselves and your marriage to bring healing. Plus, the objective counselor has the ability to dig up, point out, and put into words things you might not have known were even there. He or she can also help bridge the communication gap that might have opened up between you. If you are having problems in your marriage, whether serious issues or feelings of distance like the Eldredges experienced, be encouraged to seek counseling from your pastor or a counselor in your area. Allow for another person to speak truth into your marriage and help to pull you out of the rut you may be experiencing.

If you are not experiencing anything like this at the moment, still take to heart the advice of these couples. If you do begin to enter one of these seasons, consider seeing a counselor before you get too far into it.

Life Together

Another turning point in marriage mentioned in the video actually occurred through the course of counseling: A renewed vision of life together.

Marriage is not about two people living individual lives who happen to be sharing the same home and refrigerator. Marriage is about doing life together and having a shared vision and mission in life. Bitterness, grudges, repeated frustrations, and busyness can pull you away from this togetherness. Sometimes it takes counseling to make room to renew this. When John and Stasi were feeling distant, they went back to their honeymoon locale in Yosemite. They needed this time away to reconnect and dream together again. They needed to be reminded why they are so much better together than apart. Set aside times to renew your vision for life together.

Have you had an experience with your spouse when you have been able to get away together and reconnect? What difference did it make?

If you have already been through the earlier study session on unity, this idea of doing life together and having a shared vision may sound familiar. This important advice is worth mentioning once again here. At all points in your marriage, fight for the unity that is central to your marriage. When you are struggling to stay together and stay committed, invest time to recoup what you once had.

"A big turning point in our relationship was deciding the goal of our marriage is not two people coming together to build a happy life, a little house, and park a minivan out front. The goal of two people coming together is to be a team to fulfill a significant purpose that God has for your family." —Lysa TerKeurst

Be a team. A team is not productive if it is not working together, playing by the same rules, playing the same game, or working toward the same goal. Conflict within a team quickly destroys morale, cohesion, and motivation. However, when a team is working together, playing by the same rules, playing the same game, and working toward the same goal, it can be unstoppable. Be that team. When conflict arises, fight a good fight, work it out, repent, forgive, and commit to stick together. As you do, your marriage will continue to grow stronger and your relationship will be unstoppable.

Questions for Home

How do you handle conflict within your own marriage? What is one area you want to work on in this regard?

If you think your marriage could benefit right now from counseling, talk about this together. Practice listening to each other and your concerns.

What is your goal for marriage?

Extra: Remarriage

Today, an increasing number of couples in the church are remarried. Every marriage has its challenges and difficult seasons to navigate, and a remarriage is no different. In fact, a remarried couple is going to have a unique set of issues to work through together. Whether a previous marriage was ended by death, abuse, unfaithfulness, or any other issue, it was not an easy transition and will carry with it its own baggage that cannot be ignored. The remarried couple should keep in mind and practice the truths discussed in this study: healthy communication, personal awareness, and a no-turning-back commitment. If there are issues that continue to arise and don't seem to be resolved, then take the advice of the couples you saw in this video and seek counseling, whether together or individually. It is a small price to pay to grow individually and as a couple. In fact, counseling is an investment in your marriage as you learn more about yourselves and each other.

This bonus video has been included on the DVD for the purpose of sharing Chip and Theresa's own story of her marriage, divorce, and remarriage. They have hit roadblocks along the way—Chip being advised not to marry a divorced woman, going to counseling together, Theresa working through her lens of rejection—but the important key in their story is that they sought the Lord in their marriage and they have worked together. They have remained faithful and committed to each other as they work through their own issues. Chip and Theresa have drawn strength from their relationship with Jesus Christ, and they have encouraged and supported each other along the way.

If you are in a marriage in which one or both of you are remarried, may this story be an encouragement to you that you are not alone, and may it give you the inspiration to address areas that need to be addressed in order to grow a stronger marriage with your spouse starting now.

If you are not in a remarriage, may this video help to give you insight into one couple's journey, and may you be sensitive and aware of possible challenges others may face as you walk alongside them in love as the body of Christ.

Notes / Prayer Requests

_____

_____

_____

_____

_____

_____

_____

_____

_____

_____

_____

_____

_____

_____

_____

_____

_____

_____

_____

Notes / Prayer Requests

_____

_____

_____

_____

_____

_____

_____

_____

_____

_____

_____

_____

_____

_____

_____

_____

_____

Leader's Guide

Thank you for leading this small group for Growing a Strong Marriage! As couples gather together over the next few weeks, you have the opportunity to provide them with material that will help them to develop new ways of thinking about their marriage and themselves.

Beginning the Small Group

- The Growing a Strong Marriage series is a set of three study guides with corresponding video sessions on DVDs. Generally speaking, there is one video per session, running roughly seven to fifteen minutes each. The study guides have been developed in a way that allows the leader to customize the order of the sessions to fit the group's needs. For the most complete experience, however, it is recommended that the sessions be completed in the order in which they have been presented.

- It is recommended to keep the small groups to two to four couples in order to allow everyone adequate time to share. If you have more couples interested, encourage someone else to lead a group.

- Each session has been designed to be completed in one hour, including the video and corresponding study guide. If you have longer time to meet, you can extend the discussion or even complete two sessions back to back. If being used for a retreat, seminar, or church event, sessions can also be run one after the other.

- Lastly, please be mindful of the time. Some of the participants may have enlisted childcare in order to attend and will need to leave by a certain time. When the small group is scheduled, set a realistic time to begin and end, and do your best to hold to these times.

General Suggestions

- Some participants will be more than willing to join in discussion, while others will be more reserved. As the leader, encourage everyone to participate, respectfully guiding the talkative and drawing out the quiet. Wisely moderate when it is appropriate to allow silence for people to think and when it is best to move on to the next section of the study guide.

- As the leader, you have the opportunity to model brevity and the appropriate answer. For the first session, be the first to share when a question is asked, demonstrating proper length of response. This can also help break the ice and make others feel comfortable.

Starting the First Session

- If the participants in the small group do not already know each other or you, begin by briefly introducing yourself and asking the participants to do the same. You can cover the basics for now: names, how long married, number of children (though be sensitive to those without children), and so on. You'll go over more details of each marriage later in the session.

- Begin with prayer, asking the Lord to speak to each person and to strengthen each marriage present.

- Read through the introduction to the series and the introduction to the study guide to help introduce Growing a Strong Marriage and what the participants can expect over the next few weeks. You can either read it beforehand and summarize, or read it together as a group.

- Start with Session 1 in the study guide and then watch the session on the DVD when prompted in the guide. After you have finished watching Session 1 on the video, return to the study guide, stopping along the way to answer the discussion questions as a group.

Continuing the Following Sessions

- For each following session, open the group in prayer. Then check in with the group and see if there are any brief comments anyone has from the previous session. Be careful to leave these comments to just a few minutes so that you will have plenty of time to cover the new material.

- Begin the next session in the study guide and watch the session on the DVD when prompted in the study guide. After the video is complete, follow along in the study guide in the same way.

{ Clyde – Tristan
{ Astrid –

Marty & Mary

Caroline

Bridget
Carley ?
Eric }